PILGRIM'S PROGRESS
WORKBOOK for Kids

PILGRIM'S PROGRESS WORKBOOK for Kids

A Study Guide for *Pilgrim's Progress in Today's English*

Volume I: Christian's Journey

Caroline Weerstra

Catechism for Kids

Visit our website
www.catechismforkids.com

The solutions manual for this workbook is available for FREE download from the Catechism for Kids website.

www.catechismforkids.com

For more information on this workbook series, email:
info@catechismforkids.com

Published by Common Life Press, Schenectady, New York. 2012.

ISBN-13: 978-0983724926

This workbook is intended to accompany *Pilgrim's Progress in Today's English* by John Bunyan and James H. Thomas. All chapter titles, page numbers, characters, and other references to *Pilgrim's Progress in Today's English* are used by permission of Moody Publishers.

All Bible verses quoted in this workbook are in the New International (NIV) translation.

This workbook is a study guide intended to accompany the reading of

Pilgrim's Progress in Today's English

Authors: John Bunyan and James H. Thomas
Publisher: Moody Publishers

Contents

Introduction 5

Chapter 1: Christian in Trouble 7
- Part 1 – Christian Meets Evangelist
- Part 2 – Obstinate and Pliable
- Part 3 – The Slough of Despond
- Part 4 – Worldly Wiseman
- Part 5 – Evangelist Again

Chapter 2: Christian Returns to the Good Way 31
- Part 1 – The Gate and Goodwill
- Part 2 – The Interpreter's House (I)
- Part 3 – The Interpreter's House (II)

Chapter 3: Journey Toward the House Beautiful 45
- Part 1 – Christian Loses His Burden
- Part 2 – False Christians
- Part 3 – The Restful Arbor
- Part 4 – The House Beautiful

Chapter 4: In the Valleys of Humility and Death 65
- Part 1 – Attacked By Apollyon
- Part 2 – Horrors of the Valley of Death

Chapter 5: Christian and Faithful 75
- Part 1 – The Temptation of Faithful
- Part 2 – Discontent and Shame
- Part 3 – Talkative

Chapter 6: Vanity Fair and the City of Vanity........................... 87
- Part 1 – Vanity Fair
- Part 2 – Faithful's Trial

Chapter 7: Journey to the Delectable Mountains 97
- Part 1 – Hopeful and the Hypocrites
- Part 2 – Demas
- Part 3 – Giant Despair

Chapter 8: At the Delectable Mountains 111

Chapter 9: In the Low Country of Conceit 117
- Part 1 – Ignorance and Little-Faith
- Part 2 – The Deceiver and the Atheist
- Part 3 – Hopeful

Chapter 10: The Talk With Ignorance 129
- Part 1 – False Faith and True Faith
- Part 2 – Backsliding

Chapter 11: Near to the City of God 137

Introduction

John Bunyan's classic allegory was first published in February 1678 under the title *The Pilgrim's Progress from This Word to That Which Is to Come*. Written during a lengthy imprisonment by a man with little formal education, it nevertheless burst forth as an astounding success. It has become one of the most commonly read books of all time, and more than 300 years later, it has never been out of print.

John Bunyan's deep faith in Christ even amid great trials and suffering has inspired many generations after him. The storybook form in which he presents great theological concepts grasps the imagination of children and adults alike.

In *Pilgrim's Progress in Today's English*, James H. Thomas faithfully retells Bunyan's brilliant allegory in modern language. This is especially helpful for children, who love the story and characters of *Pilgrim's Progress* but may be discouraged by antiquated words and phrasing.

This workbook is intended as a children's study guide to accompany the reading of *Pilgrim's Progress in Today's English*. It encourages children to go beyond a simple enjoyment of the story and to think more deeply about the theological concepts underlying the characters and plot.

Each section of this workbook contains discussion of the meaning of the names of characters and the symbolism of various aspects of the story. Bible reading portions remind the readers of links between the allegory and the tenets of the Christian faith as found in Scripture. Finally, the application questions help students consider Scriptural principles in terms of real-life situations.

Pilgrim's Progress remains as relevant today as the day it was penned from the inside of a prison. The human condition persists in its error and folly, and so we catch glimpses of ourselves and those around us in the characters met by Christian and his companions on the road the Celestial City. Yet *Pilgrim's Progress* reminds us always of God's great faithfulness throughout generations, and we are encouraged to keep our eyes on Him as we travel the road of life.

Caroline Weerstra

January 6, 2012

CHAPTER 1: CHRISTIAN IN TROUBLE

PART 1: CHRISTIAN MEETS EVANGELIST
READ PAGES 11–13.

BACKGROUND

John Bunyan composed his famous tale while imprisoned for preaching the gospel. His book was first published in 1678. The original title, *The Pilgrim's Progress from This World to That Which Is to Come*, has since been simplified to *Pilgrim's Progress*.

John Bunyan was born in 1628 in Harrowden, England. His father was a tinker, so John grew up in a very poor family. He did not have much formal education, but he learned to read and write.

John Bunyan married a woman named Mary. She owned two books about God. John read the books, and he began to feel very guilty about his sins. He started going to church, and the pastor told him how to become a Christian. John later became a preacher. He told many people about God. He was even put in prison for preaching, but he never ceased proclaiming salvation in Jesus Christ.

John Bunyan wrote *Pilgrim's Progress* to help people understand salvation and Christian life. Over time, it became the most famous book in the world besides the Bible.

Pilgrim's Progress is an **allegory**.   An **allegory** is a story which illustrates important concepts.   In *Pilgrim's Progress*, people are named according to the characteristics they represent.

CHARACTERS

What do these characters' names mean?

Christian: _____

Evangelist: _____

Answer the questions below:

1. What was Christian reading that made him sad? _____

_____

2. What was Christian carrying on his back? _____

3. What did Christian fear? _____

4. How did Christian's wife and children respond when he told them how frightened he was?

_____

5. Whom did Christian meet? _____

6. Did Christian's wife and children go with him to the gate? _____

 SYMBOLISM

Christian's burden symbolizes his sin. Christian feels weighed down by the guilt of his own wickedness. Christian reads a book, which represents the law of God. People may not realize that they are doing something wrong until they begin to understand God's law. For example, a boy who cheats on his homework may not think very much about whether he is doing something wrong until he goes to church and hears his Sunday School teacher explain that cheating is a sin. Then he may be very worried. He may remember all the times he has cheated on his homework. The boy could wonder, "Have I made God angry? Is God going to punish me for all the bad things I have done?"

In the story, Christian realizes that he has sinned. He wants to be saved from his sin, but he does not know what to do. He knows that he has done wrong and that God must be angry with him, but he does not know how to be saved. Fortunately, he meets Evangelist. Evangelist tells him to leave the City of Destruction and go to the gate. The gate represents the beginning of a new life in Christ. (Opening a gate demonstrates an intention to go somewhere new.)

Christian's wife and children do not want him to follow God, but Christian knows he must do the right thing.

BIBLE READING

The apostle Paul tells us that understanding God's laws can make us realize how sinful we are:

> What shall we say, then? Is the law sin? Certainly not! Indeed, I would not have known what sin was except through the law. For I would not have known what coveting really was if the law had not said, "Do not covet." (Romans 7:7)

Paul goes on later in the same chapter to describe the agony which overtakes him when he considers how much he has sinned.

> What a wretched man I am! Who will rescue me from this body of death? (Romans 7:24)

The word **wretched** indicates misery. Paul describes how miserable he is when he considers how much he breaks God's law. He would not have even realized how much he sinned unless he had read God's rules (such as the Ten Commandments). Once he understood the law, he realized how many things he was doing wrong. He knew that he needed to be rescued from his miserable and sinful condition.

CONCLUSION

In our story, Christian (like the apostle Paul) is horrified by his sin. He needs a Savior.

Who is our Savior? _____

Evangelist helps Christian start in the right direction. Next, we will find out what happens to Christian on the way to the gate.

 REMEMBER! When we understand God's law, then we realize that we are sinners who need a Savior.

PART 2: OBSTINATE AND PLIABLE
READ PAGES 13-16.

DO YOU REMEMBER?

Christian was carrying a _____ on his back and

reading a book.   The book represents the _____ .

When he read the book, Christian realized that he was a sinner, and he

became afraid of God's judgment. He met _____

who told him to go to the _____.

CHARACTERS

What do these characters' names mean?

Obstinate: _____

Pliable: _____

Answer the questions below:

1. Why did Obstinate and Pliable chase Christian? _____

   _____

2. Did Christian agree to go back with them? _____

3. What did Christian suggest they should do? _____

   _____

4. How did Obstinate and Pliable respond when Christian suggested that they go with him?

   _____

5. How did Christian know that the words in the book were true?

   _____

6. What did Pliable want Christian to talk about? _____

 SYMBOLISM

Christian's neighbors symbolize the reactions many people have when they hear that someone has become a Christian. Some people (like Obstinate)

are stubborn and hard-hearted. They say things like, "You are crazy to believe in God!"

Some people, like Pliable, decide to follow God because it sounds very rewarding. Notice that Pliable does not seem to realize that he needs to repent of his sins. He claims to want to be a Christian, hoping to obtain better things. He likes to hear Christian talk about heaven and other pleasant topics. We will find out in the next lesson what happens when Pliable discovers that following God is not always easy.

BIBLE READING

Jesus told a story about how people respond when they hear the gospel. Let's read:

> A farmer went out to sow his seed. As he was scattering the seed, some fell along the path, and the birds came and ate it up. Some fell on rocky places, where it did not have much soil. It sprang up quickly, because the soil was shallow. But when the sun came up, the plants were scorched, and they withered because they had no root. Other seed fell among thorns, which grew up and choked the plants. Still other seed fell on good soil, where it produced a crop—a hundred, sixty or thirty times what was sown. Whoever has ears, let them hear. (Matthew 13:3-9)

Later, Jesus explained the story to his disciples.

> Listen then to what the parable of the sower means: When anyone hears the message about the kingdom and does not understand it, the evil one comes and snatches away what was sown in their heart. This is the seed sown along the path. The seed falling on rocky ground refers to someone who hears the word and at once receives it with joy. But since they have no root, they last only a short time. When trouble or persecution comes because of the word, they quickly fall away. The seed falling among the thorns refers

to someone who hears the word, but the worries of this life and the deceitfulness of wealth choke the word, making it unfruitful. But the seed falling on good soil refers to someone who hears the word and understands it. This is the one who produces a crop, yielding a hundred, sixty or thirty times what was sown. (Matthew 13:18-23)

In our story, Obstinate is like the seed which was sown along the path. Obstinate heard what Christian said, but he did not understand or accept it. Pliable accepted it quickly and very cheerfully. However, Jesus explains in the parable that not everyone who seems to accept the gospel will persevere. Sometimes people claim to want to obey God for a while, but when difficulties arise or life becomes very busy, they lose interest.

People who are truly chosen by God always **persevere**. They keep going, even amid struggles and hardships.

CONCLUSION

Suppose you tell someone that you believe in God, and they respond, "You must be CRAZY!"

This person is like _____ in our story.

Did Jesus know that some people would not accept His Word? _____

 REMEMBER! Those who are chosen by God will **accept** His Word and **persevere** in faith even when life is difficult.

PART 3: THE SLOUGH OF DESPOND
READ PAGES 17–19

DO YOU REMEMBER?

Christian was running toward the _____, and two

neighbors followed him. Their names were _____ and

_____. Christian tried to convince them to go with him.

_____ refused and returned home, but _____

decided to go with _____, because he liked the idea of going to

_____ .

CHARACTERS

What does this character's name mean?

Help: _____

Answer the questions below:

1. Why did Christian and Pliable fall into the Slough of Despond?

   _____

   _____

2. Why did Pliable go back home? _____

3. Christian asked Help why the Slough of Despond had not been repaired so that people would not fall in. What did Help tell him?

   _____

   _____

4. Was there a way around the Slough of Despond? _____

5. How did the other people back in the City of Destruction react when Pliable returned home?

   _____

   _____

SYMBOLISM

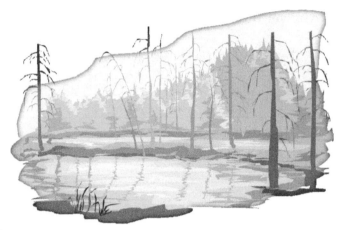

We mentioned in the last lesson that Pliable did not really understand his sinful nature or his need of a Savior. He merely had a fondness for nice things, so he liked the idea of going to heaven. When he fell into the Slough of Despond, Pliable abandoned Christian and returned home. People who are only hoping to get something pleasant from God usually do not last long in faith. When they experience difficulties, they conclude that Christian life is too hard.

The Slough of Despond symbolizes the fear and sadness which may overtake people who begin to understand their sinful nature. Perhaps they do not yet fully realize that God will forgive them, and so they are afraid and depressed. God never requires His people to feel that way. As Help told Christian, God provides everything we need to avoid falling into the swamp of despair, but people often fall in anyway because they do not pay enough attention to Scriptures about God's grace and forgiveness. People who are new to faith may not understand the Bible well, and so they are easily confused. They worry for nothing!

The conclusion to the story about Pliable illustrates the reaction of nonbelievers when someone ceases following God. These other neighbors were not obeying God, but many of them still laughed at Pliable for coming back. They could see that he only came back because of his cowardice.

These neighbors gossiped about Christian also. When people see someone else doing the right thing but do not want to change their behavior, they will try to make the right thing sound bad. For example, if one girl studies for her exam at school and achieves a good grade, and the rest of her class does not study and receives bad grades, other students might make fun of her. They do this because they are jealous. If they pretend that good grades are silly, they do not feel guilty for their laziness. Have you ever seen something like this happen?

If people laugh at you for obeying God, remember that you are still doing the right thing. Some people mock anyone who obeys God because they know they should obey God also, but they do not want to change their ways.

BIBLE READING

Jesus talked about people like Pliable who are not sure whether they want to obey God. Jesus said:

> No one who puts a hand to the plow and looks back is fit for service in the kingdom of God. (Luke 9:62)

A **plow** is a farming tool used to turn up the soil, softening it so that the farmer can plant seeds. In the old days before tractors and other machines, a farmer had to walk behind the horse or ox that pulled the plow. He had to keep his hands on the plow to hold it steady, and he had to do that all day, hour after hour, until the field was plowed and ready for planting. It was a lot of work.

Jesus declared that we must be like those farmers. We must go on steadily all day. We cannot keep changing our minds. We must **persevere**, even when we are discouraged.

CONCLUSION

Suppose someone becomes a Christian, but soon changes his or her mind as soon as life becomes difficult.

This person is like _____.

REMEMBER! God does not want us to be discouraged. Rather, we should understand that salvation is provided for us in Christ. Even if we do become discouraged, we should never give up!

PART 4: WORLDLY WISEMAN
READ PAGES 19–22

DO YOU REMEMBER?

Christian and Pliable were not careful, and so they both fell into the

_____ of _____. Pliable went back home.

Christian was pulled out by _____, who told him that there were

_____ to help people get through the swamp without falling in.

_____ was laughed at for returning home, but then

everyone spoke against _____.

CHARACTERS

What do these characters' names mean?

Worldly Wiseman: _____

Legality: _____

Answer the questions below:

1. Whom did Christian meet? _____

2. Did Worldly Wiseman think Evangelist gave Christian good advice?

   _____

3. Where did Worldly Wiseman suggest that Christian should go?

   _____

4. What did Worldly Wiseman suggest that Legality could do to help Christian?

   _____

   _____

5. Did Christian take Worldly Wiseman's suggestion? _____

6. Where did the new road lead? _____

 SYMBOLISM

Legality refers to following rules instead of trusting Christ for salvation. Worldly Wiseman symbolizes people who say, "I don't have to be a Christian! I can be a good person all on my own!"

Some people believe that they can be good without asking God to help them. It might sound like a wonderful idea at first, and people may think, "I do not have to feel bad about my sins anymore!" However, it does not work out well. We cannot be good by ourselves because we have a sinful nature. When we try to be good, we realize more and more that we are sinners.

In the Bible, Mount Sinai is the place where God gave the law to Moses. Trying to follow the law without Jesus is a hopeless endeavor. It only makes us feel more lost and afraid. The more we try to obey God's commandments, the more we realize that we need Christ to redeem us from our sins.

BIBLE READING

Do you remember reading what Paul wrote about the law of God? He said that understanding God's rules makes him realize what a terrible sinner he is.

Suppose someone thinks, "I can just stop sinning!" Can anyone succeed? Paul discussed this also:

For I know that good itself does not dwell in me, that is, in my sinful nature. For I have the desire to do what is good, but I cannot carry it out. For I do not do the good I want to do, but the evil I do not want to do—this I keep on doing. Now if I do what I do not want to do, it is no longer I who do it, but it is sin living in me that does it.

So I find this law at work: Although I want to do good, evil is right there with me. For in my inner being I delight in God's law; but I see another law at work in me, waging war against the law of my mind and making me a prisoner of the law of sin at work within me. What a wretched man I am! Who will rescue me from this body that is subject to death? Thanks be to God, who delivers me through Jesus Christ our Lord!

So then, I myself in my mind am a slave to God's law, but in my sinful nature a slave to the law of sin. (Romans 7:18-25)

Paul explained that even though he realized what he should be doing and wanted to do it, he could not. Like all of us, Paul had a sinful nature. He loved God's law, but his sinful nature kept fighting against obeying God's law. He continued doing things that he knew he should not do. We are all like Paul in this way. Sometimes we are selfish or mean, even though we want to be good and kind. We need God to help us. Paul concluded by saying thanks to God for rescuing us from our sin through Jesus Christ.

CONCLUSION

If someone says that you can be good and happy without God, are they telling the truth?

_____

What do each of us have which prevents us from being good, even when we want to be good?

_____

Was the Worldly Wiseman really wise? _____

 REMEMBER! We cannot save ourselves from sin. We need Jesus.

PART 5: EVANGELIST AGAIN
READ PAGES 22-26

DO YOU REMEMBER?

Christian was met by _____ _____, who

told him that he could have his burden removed by _____.

Christian listened and turned away from the _____, but soon he

came to _____ _____. Terrified by the fire and

danger of the mountain, Christian stopped.

CHARACTERS AND PLACES

What does this character's name mean?

Civility _____

What does this town's name mean?

Morality _____

Answer the questions below:

1. What happened when Christian started out in the direction suggested by Worldly Wiseman?

    _____

2. Why did Christian stop? _____

3. Who found Christian? _____

4. In the last paragraph of the chapter, Evangelist said that Christian had committed two sins. What were those sins?

    _____

    _____

5.   Did God forgive Christian when he repented? _____

SYMBOLISM

When Christian meets Evangelist again, he immediately feels ashamed for turning away from the gate. He knows that he was wrong to listen to Worldly Wiseman. Evangelist explains that Legality and Civility cannot help Christian. He declares them cheats and shams. He explains that merely trying to be nice is not enough. Someone can be civil (polite) to other people but still have a heart filled with sin.

Evangelist asserts that Christian sinned in two ways when he turned aside: he stopped going in the right direction, and he started going in the wrong direction. This is a reference to the idea that there are two types of sin: **sins of omission** and **sins of commission**. **Sins of omission** occur when we fail to do something which God has told us to do. Christian committed a sin of omission when he stopped going the right way. **Sins of commission** occur when we do something which God has told us not to do. Christian committed a sin of commission when he turned toward the town of Morality, which was forbidden by God.

In spite of Christian's serious sin, Evangelist encourages him that God will forgive him once he starts on the right path. Whenever we sin, we should not be discouraged. God is gracious when we repent. He forgives our sins.

BIBLE READING

In *Pilgrim's Progress*, Evangelist mentions a narrow gate. This is a direct reference to the words of Christ. Let's read what Jesus said about a narrow gate and a wide gate:

Enter through the narrow gate. For wide is the gate and broad is the road that leads to destruction, and many enter through it. But small is the gate and narrow the road that leads to life, and only a few find it. (Matthew 7:13-14)

In these verses, Jesus declares that the way to eternal life is not a wide-open field. We cannot do whatever we like and assume we will end up in heaven. God makes the way clear, but it is also very narrow. Only in Jesus do we have salvation.

The Bible relates the story of a disciple named Thomas who asked Jesus about the right way:

Thomas said to him, "Lord, we don't know where you are going, so how can we know the way?"

Jesus answered, "I am the way and the truth and the life. No one comes to the Father except through me." (John 14:5-6)

When we follow Jesus, we are on the right path. Whenever we turn away from Jesus, we are on the wrong path. The path is not wide. There are no other gods or philosophies which will give us eternal life. Salvation is found in Christ alone.

CONCLUSION

Suppose someone tells you, "You can follow the Bible, and that is fine for you. I am going to follow my own beliefs, and I will go to heaven also."

Is this true? _____

How do you know that salvation is only through Jesus? _____

_____

 REMEMBER! Salvation is found only in Christ. Other religions and philosophies will not bring someone into the right way.

CHAPTER 2: CHRISTIAN RETURNS TO THE GOOD WAY

PART 1: THE GATE AND GOODWILL
READ PAGES 27-30.

DO YOU REMEMBER?

While Christian was standing near Mount _____,

he saw _____ coming toward him.   Evangelist told him

that he had been wrong to take the advice of _____

_____ . Christian repented and Evangelist told him

that God would _____ him.

CHARACTERS

What do these characters' names mean?

Goodwill _____

Beelzebub _____

Answer the questions below:

1. What was written on the wicket gate? _____

    _____

2. Who opened the gate for Christian? _____

3. Why did Goodwill pull Christian quickly through the gate?

    _____

4. Goodwill sent Christian to follow a path. How would Christian know
    which was the right one?

    _____

 SYMBOLISM

The wicket gate symbolizes Jesus Christ. Goodwill is also a symbol of
Christ. He opens the door for those who come seeking God. The church does
not turn anyone away because God does not turn them away. When people
sincerely seek God, it is a sign that the Holy Spirit has changed their hearts. If

the Holy Spirit has chosen them, then they belong to God. We should always bring them in.

Beelzebub is a name for Satan. He tries to prevent people from finding God, so converts often need help and encouragement to begin a new Christian life.

Goodwill tells Christian that he will know the right way because it is the straight, narrow way. The path of obedience to God is quite simple. God tells us in the Bible how we can find salvation and how we can live in obedience to our Lord. People who wander off the path are usually trying to find some way around God's commandments. As long as we follow God's Word, we remain on the right path.

BIBLE READING

The wicket gate was inscribed with certain words quoted from a sermon that Jesus preached which is recorded in the gospel of Matthew:

Ask and it will be given to you; seek and you will find; knock and the door will be opened to you. For everyone who asks receives; he who seeks finds; and to him who knocks, the door will be opened. Which of you, if his son asks for bread, will give him a stone? Or if he asks for a fish, will give him a snake? If you, then, though you are evil, know how to give good gifts to your children, how much more will your Father in heaven give good gifts to those who ask him! So in everything, do to others what you would have them do to you, for this sums up the Law and the Prophets. (Matthew 7:7-14)

Jesus said that God does not turn away those who seek Him. He loves us like a father loves his children. Parents provide for their children, and God provides for us.

CONCLUSION

If someone comes to church asking to learn about God, would God ever turn that person away?

_____

Is it hard to know what God wants us to do? _____

How do we know what God wants us to do? _____

_____

 REMEMBER! Anyone who sincerely repents and asks God for salvation will receive it. He is a kind Father. He opens the door to all who knock.

PART 2: THE INTERPRETER'S HOUSE (I)
READ PAGES 31–35.

DO YOU REMEMBER?

Christian arrived at the _____ and knocked.

_____ answered. He invited Christian to come inside.

Then he pulled Christian quickly to keep him safe from _____'s

arrows. Goodwill showed Christian a _____ which would

take him to the _____ _____.

CHARACTERS

What do these characters' names mean?

Interpreter _____

Courage _____

Passion _____

Patience _____

Answer the questions below:

1. Who was the first person Interpreter showed to Christian?

   _____

2. In the second scene, a man tried to sweep a parlor but only stirred up the dust. What did the maid do?

   _____

   _____

3. What were the names of the children in the next vision?

   _____

4. In the last vision from our reading assignment, what did Courage do to get in the door?

   _____

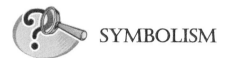

SYMBOLISM

The Interpreter's House represents the process by which we begin to know God and understand ourselves. The Interpreter shows Christian stories to explain concepts.

The first vision is merely a picture of a man who teaches people good things about God. This reminds us that we must be careful to listen to the right people—those who teach us properly.

The second lesson demonstrates that we cannot save ourselves. Interpreter illustrates this as a story of a man trying to sweep a dusty room but only stirring up the dust instead of cleaning it. The maid putting water on the dust is a symbol of the Holy Spirit changing our hearts so that we can be cleansed from sin.

The third story speaks about people who are too greedy. We must understand that we will receive our best reward in heaven. We must be patient. For example, if you want to eat a candy bar but have no money, you might be tempted to steal it to enjoy something right away. You should not be greedy. God will reward you eventually with things far better than candy bars.

The fourth story shows that God helps people persevere. The fire burns brighter even though Satan tries to put it out.

The last story discusses the necessity of courage in the Christian life. The way will not always be easy, and we might feel as though going on would be dangerous. However, God rewards those who face challenges in faith.

There are two more Interpreter stories. We will read them in the next lesson.

BIBLE READING

There are many Bible verses we could read about these things, but for now, let's focus on one. The epistle of Jude ends with this **doxology** (praise to God):

To him who is able to keep you from falling and to present you before his glorious presence without fault and with great joy — to the only God our Savior be glory, majesty, power and authority, through Jesus Christ our Lord, before all ages, now and forevermore! Amen. (Jude 1:24-25)

Like the fire burning brighter even when Satan was trying to put it out, the faith in our hearts rises even amid all Satan's attacks and life's difficulties. God is able to keep us from falling. He gives us courage to persevere.

CONCLUSION

Salvation is completely a gift from God. Our own efforts cannot save us. Which of the Interpreter's stories illustrates this?

_____

_____

God does not save us and then leave us. He provides us with the strength to persevere in faith. Which of the Interpreter's stories illustrates this?

_____

REMEMBER! We should be brave, patient, and careful. However, we should also be confident that God will preserve our faith even amid difficulties.

PART 3: THE INTERPRETER'S HOUSE (II)
READ PAGES 35–38.

DO YOU REMEMBER?

Christian followed the path to the _____'s House.

The _____ showed Christian stories to help him

learn about faith. The first lesson was a _____ of a man who

would teach him. The second vision was a man sweeping a _____ ,

and a _____ put water on the dust to make it settle. The third

story concerned two children named _____ and

_____ . The fourth was a _____ that would

not burn out. Then he showed Christian a man named _____

fighting his way into a _____ .

CHARACTERS

What do these characters' names mean?

Interpreter _____

Hopeless_____

Loveworld _____

Answer the questions below:

1. Where was Hopeless? _____

2. Why was Hopeless sad? _____

_____

3. What dream did Loveworld have? _____

_____

_____

 # SYMBOLISM

The last two lessons Christian learns at Interpreter's House are warnings. The first concerns a man who has lost hope in his salvation. The man believes that the Holy Spirit has left him and that he cannot be accepted by God anymore. The second is a man who has dreamed that he is not ready for judgment and will be sent to hell.

Hopeless hardened his heart so much that he no longer wants to repent. Even though his sin makes him miserable, he will not return to Christ. He is trapped by his own foolishness. He even wants to leave his sin, but he cannot seem to want it enough to change his ways.

Loveworld's name indicates that he places all his affection on things of the world. In the end, the world will be destroyed, and he will lose everything, including his own soul.

These stories serve as warnings for Christian and also for us. We must remember that salvation is very important. We must not turn aside from God and think we will repent later. Some people who put off repenting become too hardened in their sin to change at all, and some people find that the end comes too suddenly for them to change their minds.

 # BIBLE READING

The book of Revelation speaks of people who fear God's judgment:

Then the kings of the earth, the princes, the generals, the rich, the mighty, and everyone else, both slave and free, hid in caves and among the rocks of the mountains. They called to the mountains and the rocks, "Fall on us and hide us from the face of him who sits on the throne and from the wrath of the

Lamb! For the great day of their wrath has come, and who can withstand it?" (Revelation 6:15-17)

This Bible passage speaks of kings, princes, generals, rich and powerful people hiding in the caves and among the rocks alongside everyone else. Earthly power will not matter when people see God. The wicked will never stand against God's judgment. They will run and hide, asking that even the rocks would fall on them to hide them from God.

CONCLUSION

Read Matthew 16:25-26. Copy it here:

_____

_____

_____

_____

 REMEMBER! Nothing is more important than salvation. There is nothing on earth worth losing our souls.

CHAPTER 3: JOURNEY TOWARD THE HOUSE BEAUTIFUL

PART 1: CHRISTIAN LOSES HIS BURDEN
READ PAGES 39-40.

DO YOU REMEMBER?

Christian saw two last warning stories at the _____'s

House. A man called _____ had lost hope of being

saved. He did not want to _____ of his sins. Another man

_____ was troubled by a dream about God's judgment at

the end of the _____.

Answer the questions below:

1. Where did Christian finally lose his burden? _____

_____

2. Why did Christian weep? _____

3. What did the celestial beings give to Christian? _____

_____

 ## SYMBOLISM

Christian finally loses his burden of sin when he sees the cross. When he understands that Jesus died on the cross and paid the penalty for his sins, he realizes that he does not have to bear the punishment for sin. His old sinful nature died, and he has been raised up to a new life in Christ.

Christian receives new clothes, a mark on his forehead, and a book from the celestial beings. These represent new life in Jesus. When we are forgiven and accepted through Christ, God adopts us as His children. He makes our hearts new and clean. Baptism marks us as people who belong to God.

BIBLE READING

In the book of Romans, Paul talks about dying to our old sinful nature and rising to new life in Christ:

> What shall we say, then? Shall we go on sinning so that grace may increase? By no means! We are those who have died to sin; how can we live in it any longer? Or don't you know that all of us who were baptized into Christ Jesus were baptized into his death? We were therefore buried with

him through baptism into death in order that, just as Christ was raised from the dead through the glory of the Father, we too may live a new life.

For if we have been united with him in a death like his, we will certainly also be united with him in a resurrection like his. For we know that our old self was crucified with him so that the body ruled by sin might be done away with, that we should no longer be slaves to sin—because anyone who has died has been set free from sin.

Now if we died with Christ, we believe that we will also live with him. For we know that since Christ was raised from the dead, he cannot die again; death no longer has mastery over him. The death he died, he died to sin once for all; but the life he lives, he lives to God. (Romans 6:1-10)

Paul explains that we are saved by God's grace to us. God washes us clean from sin so that it is like we never sinned at all. However, we should certainly not continue carelessly sinning. Our old sinful nature has died.

Jesus rose from the dead, and we are also raised up. We are not slaves to sin anymore; we are free. We have a new nature in Christ. We may still sin sometimes, but we now want to be pure. We ask God to forgive us and to help us to refrain from sinning. We pray that God would make us holy.

Baptism represents the death of old self and resurrection with Christ. Through our baptism, God assures us that we are marked as His people.

CONCLUSION

What is the mark by which everyone knows that we belong to God?

Have you been baptized? If so, when? _____

What happens when you are baptized? _____

_____

What does baptism represent? _____

_____

 REMEMBER! God forgives our sins and gives us new life in Christ. We are not slaves to sin anymore. We belong to God.

PART 2: FALSE CHRISTIANS
READ PAGES 40–44.

DO YOU REMEMBER?

When Christian saw the cross on the hill, his _____

fell off his back and rolled into a _____. Three celestial beings

appeared. They gave Christian new _____, a _____

on his forehead, and a _____ to read and for identification at the

Celestial _____.

CHARACTERS

What do these characters' names mean?

Simple _____

Sloth _____

Presumption _____

Formality _____

Hypocrisy _____

Answer the questions below:

1. What were Simple, Sloth, and Presumption doing when Christian saw them?

_____

2. When Christian tried to warn Simple, Sloth, and Presumption of their danger, how did they respond?

_____

_____

3. How did Formality and Hypocrisy arrive at the path?

_____

_____

4. What happened when Formality and Hypocrisy reached the Hill of Difficulty?

_____

_____

 SYMBOLISM

In this portion of *Pilgrim's Progress*, John Bunyan explains that there are people who claim to be Christians but do not really love God. In the story, Christian encounters three men who are in chains and asleep. He tries to warn them and offers to free them, but they fall back to sleep again. Simple is too foolish to understand his peril. Sloth is too lazy to do anything about it. Presumption does not think it matters. These all represent people who ignore God's commands and make no effort to live as faithful Christians.

The next two people met by Christian are Formality and Hypocrisy. These represent people who make an outward show of being Christians, but they have no real intention of obeying God when life becomes hard. These men could not even take the trouble to begin their journey the right way. Instead of entering at the gate, they climbed in over the wall. Therefore, they failed to go to the cross, which shows that they never really repented of their sins at all.

Formality and Hypocrisy appear to be making excellent progress along the path until they encounter a difficult hill, and then they decide to try to go their own way. People who are insincere in their repentance never remain faithful to God in hard times. When they find Christianity too troublesome, they quickly fall away. In the end, they return to their sins.

Christian was able to avoid destruction because he remained on the right path. He continued to be obedient to God even during difficulty, and so he was spared from destruction.

BIBLE READING

The Bible tells us that God hates **hypocrisy** (the pretense of service to God while living in great disobedience). In ancient Judah, people commonly went up to Jerusalem to offer sacrifices at the temple of the Lord even after committing serious sins at home. They pretended to honor God, but they were not obeying God's commands.

God sent the prophet Jeremiah to speak to the people as they were on their way into the temple to offer sacrifices:

This is what the LORD Almighty, the God of Israel, says: Reform your ways and your actions, and I will let you live in this place. Do not trust in deceptive words and say, "This is the temple of the LORD, the temple of the LORD, the temple of the LORD!" If you really change your ways and your actions and deal with each other justly, if you do not oppress the foreigner, the fatherless or the widow and do not shed innocent blood in this place, and if you do not follow other gods to your own harm, then I will let you live in this place, in the land I gave your ancestors for ever and ever. But look, you are trusting in deceptive words that are worthless. Will you steal and murder, commit adultery and perjury, burn incense to Baal and follow other gods you have not known, and then come and stand before me in this house, which bears my Name, and say, "We are safe"—safe to do all these detestable things? Has this house, which bears my Name, become a den of robbers to you? But I have been watching! declares the LORD. (Jeremiah 7:3-11)

God warned the people of Judah that they should treat people fairly, be kind to the poor, honor God, and refrain from murdering innocent people. These things seem obvious, and yet the people of Judah imagined that they could get away with killing and hurting other people if they offered sacrifices to God at the temple! God was very angry. He warned them that they could not do horrible things and then stand in the house of God.

Just as Hypocrisy and Formality thought they could get in over the wall, some people today still think they can do whatever evil things they want to do and then go to church. This is wrong. Like Hypocrisy and Formality, they will be judged for their disobedience to God's commands.

CONCLUSION

Why was God angry with the people of Judah who were coming to offer sacrifices in the temple?

_____

What sins were the people of Judah committing at home before they came up to the temple pretending to honor God?

_____

_____

How does God want us to honor him?

_____

_____

REMEMBER! It is not enough to attend church. God requires us to sincerely repent of our sins and to honor Him every day at home, school, and wherever else we go. God can see us everywhere.

PART 3: THE RESTFUL ARBOR
READ PAGES 44-47.

DO YOU REMEMBER?

Christian saw three sleeping men with _____ on their

feet. Their names were _____, _____, and

_____ . He tried to warn them, but they would not listen.

Later, he also met _____ and _____,

who had reached the path by climbing over the _____ . They were

sure that they could get to the _____ City their own way,

but when they came to the _____ of _____, they

tried to go around, and they were both _____.

CHARACTERS

What do these characters' names mean?

Timorous _____

Mistrust _____

Watchful _____

Answer the questions below:

1. What did Christian lose in the arbor? _____

2. Why were Mistrust and Timorous running away? _____

    _____

    _____

3. How did Christian find his book again? _____

    _____

4. How was Christian able to pass by the lions without being eaten?

SYMBOLISM

Christian fell asleep in the arbor and lost his book. This event represents the tendency for Christians to become lazy and undisciplined. Sometimes people stop reading their Bibles. Maybe they still love God and know they should read Scripture, but they become sluggish and do not put in the effort. As long as life continues going well, they may not think about it much. When trouble comes, suddenly they realize that they do not know the Bible as well as they should.

If we realize that we have become too complacent and slothful, then the only proper thing to do is to start again—read the Bible, pray, and do the daily things which we were supposed to be doing all along.

Because he trusted God, Christian was able to walk between the lions. Mistrust and Timorous did not believe God's promises to protect them, and so they ran away. Christian was afraid, but he continued on the right way. Sometimes we also must continue obeying God, even when we are frightened. We must believe and trust in God.

BIBLE READING

When Christian was asleep in the Restful Arbor, he was awakened by a voice telling him something about an ant. Do you remember what the voice said? It was quoting a Bible verse from the book of Proverbs. Let's read it:

Go to the ant, you sluggard; consider its ways and be wise! It has no commander, no overseer or ruler, yet it stores its provisions in summer and gathers its food at harvest. (Proverbs 6:6-8)

Have you ever watched ants? What do you see them doing? They are always working! They walk in lines, collecting food and bringing it back to the anthill. Ants store food so that they will always have plenty to eat.

God tells us that we should be wise like ants. We should work hard and prepare for difficult times. This is true in every part of life. At school, you should study hard so that you will be ready for exams. At home, you should wash your clothes so that you will have something clean to wear. This is also true in Christian faith. We should pray and read our Bibles every day so that we are well-prepared.

CONCLUSION

An ant works every day storing food for winter. Draw a picture of something you do that is hard work:

REMEMBER! Christian life often requires hard work and trust in the Lord. We should remember that difficult times are ahead. We should not be lazy about praying and reading our Bibles.

PART 4: THE HOUSE BEAUTIFUL
READ PAGES 47–55.

DO YOU REMEMBER?

Christian fell asleep in the arbor and lost his _____. He

met _____ and _____, who warned him

to go back because of the _____ ahead.

Christian realized he had lost his _____, and he had to

return to the _____ to get it.   He went on, and as he approached the

_____, he was afraid. _____ told him to go

straight ahead. He arrived safely at the _____ _____.

CHARACTERS

What do these characters' names mean?

Discretion _____

Prudence _____

Piety _____

Charity _____

Answer the questions below:

1. Prudence asked Christian whether he still thought of the place that he had come from. What did Christian answer?

    _____

    _____

2. Charity asked Christian whether he had tried to persuade his wife and children to join him on the path to the Celestial City. What did Christian say?

    _____

    _____

3. What did Christian see in the armory? _____

_____

4. What did Christian's friends at the House Beautiful give him to take on his journey?

_____

SYMBOLISM

Christian is approaching the Valley of Humility. Before he arrives, he stops for a while at the House Beautiful. He rests and talks with other believers and learns stories of heroes of faith. This helps him prepare for the rest of the journey.

God provides for us in a similar way. We can be encouraged through fellowship with other Christians. We are built up in our faith and prepared for trials when we remember that other people have been through difficulties and were strong in the Lord.

BIBLE READING

The Bible tells us many stories of faithful people. Hebrews 11 is a famous Bible chapter with a remarkable list of heroes. Let's read a portion of this chapter and remember the stories:

By faith Abel brought God a better offering than Cain did. By faith he was commended as righteous, when God spoke well of his offerings. And by faith Abel still speaks, even though he is dead.

By faith Enoch was taken from this life, so that he did not experience death: "He could not be found, because God had taken him away." For before he was taken, he was commended as one who pleased God. And without faith it is impossible to please God, because anyone who comes to him must believe that he exists and that he rewards those who earnestly seek him.

By faith Noah, when warned about things not yet seen, in holy fear built an ark to save his family. By his faith he condemned the world and became heir of the righteousness that is in keeping with faith.

By faith Abraham, when called to go to a place he would later receive as his inheritance, obeyed and went, even though he did not know where he was going. By faith he made his home in the promised land like a stranger in a foreign country; he lived in tents, as did Isaac and Jacob, who were heirs with him of the same promise. For he was looking forward to the city with foundations, whose architect and builder is God. (Hebrews 11:4-10)

Nobody listed in Hebrews 11 was perfect. They were all people like you and me. They believed God, and so they obeyed him. You are called to do the same. Put your faith in God, just like Abel, Enoch, Noah, Abraham, and all the other faithful believers throughout history!

CONCLUSION

Read the rest of Hebrews 11. List three other heroes of faith mentioned in this chapter.

Who is your favorite Bible hero? _____

There are many heroes of faith mentioned in the Bible, of course. There are heroes of faith today as well, even in everyday life. All Christians can be heroes for each other, building one another up in faith. Can you think of a time when someone helped you understand the Bible or resist temptation?

Who has helped you be faithful to God? _____

 REMEMBER! God provides Christian friends for us so that we may be encouraged to be strong in faith.

CHAPTER 4: IN THE VALLEYS OF HUMILITY AND DEATH

> ## PART 1: ATTACKED BY APOLLYON
> ### READ PAGES 56–60.

DO YOU REMEMBER?

Christian arrived at the _____ _____,

where he _____. Before Christian continued his journey, the ladies of

the house gave him _____ from the armory. The Porter told him

that a man named _____ had passed by on the path.

CHARACTERS

What does this character's name mean?

Apollyon _____

Answer the questions below:

1. What had Apollyon once own which he had lost? _____

    _____

2. How did Apollyon say that Christian had been unfaithful to his new King?

    _____

    _____

3. How did Christian block the flaming darts thrown by Apollyon?

    _____

4. How did Christian finally win the battle?

    _____

 SYMBOLISM

Apollyon is the destroyer. He represents Satan. Just as Christian had once been a servant of Apollyon, so also we were once slaves to sin, but now we have been set free to serve God.

We are sometimes attacked by Satan, like Apollyon attacked Christian. If we listen to him, Satan will tempt us to doubt God's love. We should remember the promises of God, so that Satan will not destroy our faith.

BIBLE READING

The Bible describes the weapons which God provides for us in the battle against Satan:

> Put on the full armor of God, so that you can take your stand against the devil's schemes. For our struggle is not against flesh and blood, but against the rulers, against the authorities, against the powers of this dark world and against the spiritual forces of evil in the heavenly realms. Therefore put on the full armor of God, so that when the day of evil comes, you may be able to stand your ground, and after you have done everything, to stand. Stand firm then, with the belt of truth buckled around your waist, with the breastplate of righteousness in place, and with your feet fitted with the readiness that comes from the gospel of peace. In addition to all this, take up the shield of faith, with which you can extinguish all the flaming arrows of the evil one. Take the helmet of salvation and the sword of the Spirit, which is the word of God. (Ephesians 6:11-17)

In this letter to the church at Ephesus, Paul explains that we are not fighting against people, but rather we battle against Satan and his demons. Our weapons are not guns and knives. Instead, we fight in a spiritual way.

God has given us the truth and righteousness of Christ, which defends us against Satan's accusations and temptations. We are further protected by the gospel of peace by which we are reconciled to God. We have the shield of faith—we trust God and so we are not destroyed when Satan tempts us to doubt God. The Bible assures us that God loves us and forgives our sins.

When we have been reading and learning Scripture, we are well-prepared to defend ourselves against any attack of Satan.

CONCLUSION

Jesus was tempted by Satan in the desert. The story is told to us in Matthew 4:1-11. Read the story and answer the questions below.

How many times was Jesus tempted by Satan? _____

How did Jesus use the sword of the Spirit (the Word of God) against Satan?

_____

_____

REMEMBER! Satan tries to make us doubt God or tempts us to disobey God, but we can stand strong and use the weapons provided by God: truth, righteousness, the gospel, faith, salvation, and the Word of God.

PART 2: HORRORS OF THE VALLEY OF DEATH
READ PAGES 60-65.

DO YOU REMEMBER?

A monster named _____ attacked Christian on the

path. He tempted Christian to doubt God. Christian's _____

protected him against Apollyon's darts, and he used his _____

to defeat the monster. Christian was injured, but he used _____

leaves to heal his wounds.

CHARACTERS

What do these characters' names mean?

Self-Love _____

Critic _____

Pope _____

Pagan _____

Answer the questions below:

1. Why did Self-Love and Critic tell Christian to turn back?

    _____

2. What weapon did Christian have against the voices which he heard?

    _____

3. What did the demon do to torment Christian?

    _____

    _____

4. Why did the giants Pope and Pagan leave Christian alone?

    _____

    _____

SYMBOLISM

The Valley of the Shadow of Death indicates a time of severe trial and suffering. When we see terrible difficulties ahead of us, we naturally tend to run away like Self-Love and Critic. We might think that God should not send these troubling problems into our lives. We may even begin to doubt Him.

Christian proceeds ahead, however, and he is soon on a narrow path lined by ditches on either side. He hears terrible dangers around him, and he is very afraid. A demon sneaks up behind him to whisper blasphemy into his ear. During severe trials, Satan often takes advantage of the bad situation to torment us. Satan troubles our minds to drive us into despair. We must continue straight ahead and trust that God will be with us.

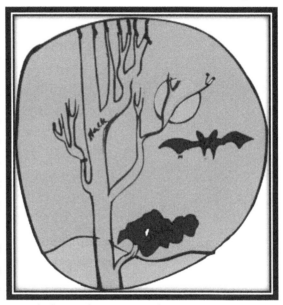

As Christian emerges from the Valley of the Shadow of Death, he glimpses the pile of skeletons left by Pagan and Pope. The giants do not attack him, however, because Pagan is dead and Pope is old and toothless. John Bunyan uses these giants as symbols of great enemies of Christianity in the past. Pagans (who worship other gods) and the pope (the head of the Roman Catholic Church) had caused the death and destruction of many Christians in history. However, by the time John Bunyan wrote his story, paganism had ceased to exist to any large extent in Europe, and the pope had lost much of his authority.

BIBLE READING

King David wrote a beautiful psalm about God's provision for us during times of great trial. He pictured God as a Shepherd watching over sheep. Sometimes the Shepherd leads us along dark and frightening paths, but we do not need to be afraid. He is with us. He gives us everything we need.

Psalm 23

The LORD is my shepherd, I lack nothing.
He makes me lie down in green pastures,
he leads me beside quiet waters,
he refreshes my soul.
He guides me along the right paths
for his name's sake.
Even though I walk
through the darkest valley,
I will fear no evil,
for you are with me;
your rod and your staff,
they comfort me.
You prepare a table before me
in the presence of my enemies.
You anoint my head with oil;
my cup overflows.
Surely your goodness and love will follow me
all the days of my life,
and I will dwell in the house of the LORD
forever.

CONCLUSION

When we are afraid and feel alone, what should we remember?

Does God ever lead us through difficult times? _____

God promises that He will never leave us. Look up Hebrews 13:5 in your
Bible and copy it here:

_____

_____

_____

_____

 REMEMBER! Sometimes God leads us through great trials, but He
is always with us.

CHAPTER 5: CHRISTIAN AND FAITHFUL

PART 1: THE TEMPTATION OF FAITHFUL
READ PAGES 66-72.

DO YOU REMEMBER?

Christian entered the Valley of the _____ of _____,

in spite of the warnings of _____ and _____.

Christian was frightened by the horrors in the valley, and a _____

tormented him by whispering _____ in his ear.

Christian was encouraged when he heard a _____, and he

was able to travel safely through the valley. As he was leaving the valley, he

saw the destruction left by two giants _____ and _____ ,

but they did not _____ him.

CHARACTERS

What do these characters' names mean?

Faithful _____

Wanton _____

Answer the questions below:

1. What happened to Pliable after he returned to the City of Destruction?

    _____

2. Wanton tempted Faithful. How did he respond? _____

    _____

3. What was the name of the old man who offered to give Faithful his house as an inheritance?

    _____

4. Why did Faithful refuse the old man's offer?

    _____

5. What did the old man do when Faithful refused to go with him?

_____

_____

 ## SYMBOLISM

Faithful was tempted to live an easy, self-centered life seeking only after pleasure. With the help of God, he was able to resist this temptation. He was first enticed by a wicked woman. She offered him fleshly pleasure, but God helped Faithful remember that he should not defile his body. Then Faithful was tempted by Adam the First, who offered to help him gather wealth and enjoy luxury. He escaped when he realized that he would be a slave to the old man, but he was tormented still by the commandments he had broken. Christ saved Faithful from being destroyed by the law.

We are all tempted to live only for the pleasures and wealth of this world. We must remember that obeying God is more important than anything in life. People who live only for money and pleasure soon become slaves to it. They can never get enough to make them happy; they are always discontent. We should keep this in mind so that we will not be ensnared by temptation.

Whenever we do break God's commandments, we should remember that Christ died for us. Guilt would destroy us unless Jesus had taken the penalty for our sins.

BIBLE READING

Jesus instructed us to remember that worldly possessions do not last forever:

> Do not store up for yourselves treasures on earth, where moths and vermin destroy, and where thieves break in and steal. But store up for yourselves treasures in heaven, where moths and vermin do not destroy, and where thieves do not break in and steal. For where your treasure is, there your heart will be also. (Matthew 6:19-21)

We must always remember that loving God is the most important thing in life. Sometimes we are tempted to ignore God and seek after pleasure, money, or popularity. These Bible verses remind us that all those things are temporary. Eventually, we all die, and we cannot take anything with us. Only our obedience to God bears eternal fruit.

CONCLUSION

Suppose someone says to you, "I do not have time to read my Bible or go to church. I want a nice house and a nice car, and so I have to focus on earning more money right now. Someday, I will have time to think about God."

How would you respond?

_____

_____

_____

 REMEMBER! The world is passing away. God is eternal, and we should love Him more than anything else.

PART 2: DISCONTENT AND SHAME
READ PAGES 73–76.

DO YOU REMEMBER?

Christian caught up with _____ on the path. Faithful

told Christian his story. He said that he had been tempted by _____

and by _____ the First, both of whom promised pleasures of this life.

Later, Faithful had been beaten by _____ for breaking the law, but

he was rescued by _____.

CHARACTERS

What does these characters' names mean?

Discontent _____

Shame _____

Answer the questions below:

1. Why was Discontent unhappy on his journey?

   _____

   _____

2. What was Shame's opinion of sermons?

   _____

3. What did Shame think about asking forgiveness?

   _____

4. In his conversation with Shame, what did Faithful say would be crucial on the day of judgment?

   _____

 SYMBOLISM

Discontent and Shame represent temptations in Christian life. We all have a tendency to be discontent and arrogant. Our dissatisfaction can lead us to complain that we are not important enough or that others are not

paying enough attention to us. Pride can make us embarrassed to obey God. For example, when we do something wrong, we should confess it and ask forgiveness, even if we are embarrassed and do not feel like apologizing.

Faithful was not deceived by Discontent or Shame, and yet Christian noted that everyone should still be cautious, especially concerning Shame. Our pride is always a danger in Christian life. We must always guard against it and remind ourselves to be humble in our obedience to God.

 ## BIBLE READING

Proud people never think they need to learn anything. They are easily angered and do not want to apologize to anyone. They resist God's authority over them.

Humility enables us to learn. When we are humble, we think more about others than about ourselves. We apologize when we hurt other people, and we confess our sins to God.

The Bible tells us repeatedly that God loves the humble. This passage in the book of Psalms explains why humility is important:

Good and upright is the LORD; therefore he instructs sinners in his ways. He guides the humble in what is right and teaches them his way. All the ways of the LORD are loving and faithful toward those who keep the demands of his covenant. (Psalm 25:8-10)

Humble people never forget that they are sinners. They do not think too highly of themselves, and so they listen to God's instructions. The Lord guides them in what is right.

CONCLUSION

Alexis's mother reminded her before school, "Don't forget your homework!" Alexis tried to remember, but, as she was leaving school, she started talking to her friends. She was already on the bus when she remembered that she had left her homework in her desk.

If Alexis is **proud**, how do you think she will answer when her mother asks about her homework?

_____

_____

If Alexis is **humble**, how do you think she will answer when her mother asks about her homework?

_____

_____

 REMEMBER! We must be humble before God, remembering that we are sinners. We must listen to His instruction in the Bible.

PART 3: TALKATIVE
READ PAGES 76-86.

DO YOU REMEMBER?

Faithful told _____ more about his adventures on the

path. Faithful had met _____, who complained that there was

no dignity in being a believer. Later, Faithful met _____, who

thought humility was embarrassing. Faithful told him that we should not

think too much about other people's opinions because _____ will

be our judge on the day of _____.

CHARACTERS

What does this character's name mean?

Talkative _____

Answer the questions below:

1. What did Faithful think about Talkative at first? _____

   _____

2. What was Christian's warning? _____

   _____

3. How did Talkative respond when Faithful started asking him about his behavior?

   _____

   _____

4. What was the problem with Talkative? _____

   _____

 SYMBOLISM

The character of Talkative symbolizes a person who is able to say all the right things about God but does not live according to God's law.

Talkative is so persuasive that Faithful initially believes him to be a sincere follower of God. Christian sees through the deception only because he already knows Talkative and has seen his behavior on prior occasions.

It can be difficult to recognize a hypocrite right away. Hypocrites can be very good at pretending to love God. The difference between a sincere Christian and a hypocrite is best discovered in their behavior. A person who really loves God will endeavor to obey God. A hypocrite merely wants to be popular, and so he only speaks and acts like a Christian among other Christians. At home or at work, he does not obey God.

BIBLE READING

The book of James talks about people who claim to have faith in God and yet do not obey God. Let's read the Bible passage:

What good is it, my brothers and sisters, if someone claims to have faith but has no deeds? Can such faith save them? Suppose a brother or a sister is without clothes and daily food. If one of you says to them, "Go in peace; keep warm and well fed," but does nothing about their physical needs, what good is it? In the same way, faith by itself, if it is not accompanied by action, is dead. (James 2:14-17)

James declares that talk is empty and worthless if someone does not also obey God. It would be like saying to a hungry person, "Don't be hungry anymore," but failing to offer any food. What good is the talk? It is worthless!

It is also worthless to talk about obeying God without actual obedience. Faith must be accompanied by actions.

CONCLUSION

Read John 14:15 and copy it here:

_____

_____

 REMEMBER! Real faith is always accompanied by real obedience to God.

CHAPTER 6: VANITY FAIR AND THE CITY OF VANITY

PART 1: VANITY FAIR
READ PAGES 87–93.

DO YOU REMEMBER?

Christian and Faithful met _____ on the path.

Faithful liked _____ at first, but Christian recollected him

as someone who liked to _____ but did not obey _____

in his everyday _____ .

PLACES

What does this town name mean?

Vanity _____

Answer the questions below:

1. Whom did Christian and Faithful meet again? _____

2. What warning did Evangelist give them? _____

_____

3. What did the people of Vanity care about?

_____

4. Who built Vanity Fair? _____

5. Why were Christian and Faithful arrested? _____

_____

 SYMBOLISM

Vanity Fair symbolizes all the distractions Satan uses to turn our hearts away from God. **Vanity** indicates worthlessness, and all the things bought and sold at the fair are ultimately worthless. Thieves and liars abound at Vanity Fair, hawking useless entertainment and merchandise. John Bunyan notes that the town is so big that no one can avoid it. Every Christian will be tempted by the vain things of the earth.

The world is indeed filled with worthless things and people who want to defraud others. It is easy to get caught up in the pursuit of vanity.

When Christian and Faithful refuse to buy anything from Vanity Fair, the citizens of Vanity City are enraged. They riot, and ultimately, Christian and Faithful are arrested, mocked, and mistreated.

People who indulge in worthless pursuits often become upset with anyone who will not join them. In their hearts, they know that they are doing wrong, but they do not want to repent. Instead, they mock and rage against anyone who turns away from vanity.

Evangelist warns Christian and Faithful that bad things will happen to them in Vanity Fair, but he also reminds them to be courageous and to be faithful to Christ Jesus. This is good advice for us as well. There is no way to be certain that everyone will be nice to us. However, we must resolve to be faithful to God no matter what happens, trusting in God for strength.

BIBLE READING

In his discussion with Christian and Faithful, Evangelist quotes several Scripture passages. The Bible is always our best comfort in times of trial, so Evangelist reminds Christian and Faithful of the Word of God as they are heading into great difficulty. Let's read one of the Bible passages quoted in this section:

> Do not be deceived: God cannot be mocked. A man reaps what he sows. Whoever sows to please their flesh, from the flesh will reap destruction; whoever sows to please the Spirit, from the Spirit will reap eternal life. Let us not become weary in doing good, for at the proper time we will reap a harvest if we do not give up. Therefore, as we have opportunity, let us do good to all people, especially to those who belong to the family of believers. (Galatians 6:7-10)

In this passage, Paul encourages the church at Galatia to be faithful to Christ. He tells them that, if they do not give up, they will ultimately be glad that they continued to do good. Those people who fill their lives with worthless things are destroying themselves. God rewards those who obey Him.

CONCLUSION

Matt and David were in the same class in school. One day, David asked Matt to go to the store with him. Matt was glad that David wanted to be his friend. However, when they arrived at the store, David took some baseball cards from the shelf and whispered, "Put these in your pockets! I will distract the clerk so he won't see you, and then we can sneak out of the store without paying!"

"I don't want to steal anything," said Matt. "Let's just save up our money to buy some baseball cards."

"You are a sissy!" David hissed. He stormed out of the store, and the next day, he would not speak to Matt at all. He told the other boys in the class that Matt was a sissy, and soon no one would speak to Matt.

Matt wondered if he had done the right thing by refusing to help David steal. "I was trying to obey God," Matt thought. "But now everyone thinks I am a sissy."

What would you tell Matt? _____

_____

Suppose David continues to steal from the store. Do you think he will always get away with his stealing? What do you think will happen eventually?

_____

_____

REMEMBER! Never get tired of doing good things. God rewards those who obey him.

PART 2: FAITHFUL'S TRIAL
READ PAGES 93–98.

DO YOU REMEMBER?

Christian and Faithful met _____ again. He warned

them that they would soon arrive at a town called _____ and

suffer greatly there. When Christian and _____ arrived in

the city, they were _____ because they refused to buy vanities.

CHARACTERS

What do these characters' names mean?

Lord Hategood _____

Mr. Envy _____

Mr. Supersition _____

Mr. Deception _____

Answer the questions below:

1. What was Mr. Envy's accusation against Faithful?

    _____

2. What was Mr. Superstition's accusation against Faithful?

    _____

3. What was Mr. Deception's accusation against Faithful?

    _____

4. What happened to Faithful?

    _____

5.   What happened to Christian after Faithful was killed?

    _____

 SYMBOLISM

John Bunyan wrote *Pilgrim's Progress* while he was imprisoned for preaching the gospel. It is likely that he derived his description of the trial and witnesses from his own experience with injustice which condemned him for the "crime" of preaching the Word of God.

Although most of us today have never been in prison for our faith, we still face more subtle pressure from those around us. We may be judged unfairly. People might accuse us of being disruptive simply because we will not join them in their wickedness. People may even tell lies about us, as Mr. Deceptive did about Faithful. Whatever happens to us, we must remain faithful to God. Never trade your heavenly reward for worldly vanities.

BIBLE READING

In the gospel of Matthew, Jesus reminds us of the great value of our souls. He asks:

> What good will it be for someone to gain the whole world, yet forfeit their soul? Or what can anyone give in exchange for their soul? For the Son of Man is going to come in his Father's glory with his angels, and then he will reward each person according to what they have done. (Matthew 16:26-27)

Nothing is worth losing our souls. Even if we could gain everything in the world, it would all be vanity. In the end, God rewards the righteous and condemns the wicked.

CONCLUSION

What sort of things were people buying at Vanity Fair?

_____

_____

In order to purchase their vanities, the people of the town were giving up their souls. Was this a good exchange?

_____

At the end of the chapter, Christian sang a song about Faithful which ended with these words: *Though they killed you, you are still alive.* What does this mean?

_____

_____

_____

 REMEMBER! Nothing is worth more than your soul.

CHAPTER 7: JOURNEY TO THE DELECTABLE MOUNTAINS

PART 1: HOPEFUL AND THE HYPOCRITES
READ PAGES 99–107.

DO YOU REMEMBER?

In the town of Vanity, _____ was put on trial. The

witnesses against him were Mr. _____, Mr. _____,

and Mr. _____ . Evil men killed _____ and

put _____ in prison. Christian was eventually released,

and he continued on his way, singing about _____.

CHARACTERS

What do these characters' names mean?

Hopeful _____

Crafty _____

Moneylove _____

Earthy _____

Save-All _____

Answer the questions below:

1. What did Hopeful tell Christian about Faithful's death?

   _____

2. Why did Christian refuse to allow Crafty to travel with him?

   _____

3. Where had Crafty, Earthy, Moneylove, and Save-All attended school?

   _____

4. What most interested Crafty, Earthy, Moneylove, and Save-All?

   _____

SYMBOLISM

In this reading section, John Bunyan continues to impress upon his readers the value of souls. Hopeful's conversion occurs as a result of Faithful's death. Hearing the news, Christian knows that Faithful's death was not empty or useless. Faithful paid a terrible price, but his death brought something wonderful and eternally valuable.

The tale continues as Christian and Hopeful meet Crafty, Save-All, Earthy, and Moneylove. These men all profess to follow God, but they are most interested in the material things they might acquire. They believe that Christianity may help them obtain more things. Christian is horrified by the suggestion. He has seen his friend Faithful give up everything (even his own life) for Christ, and he recognizes that faith is not about receiving more money or other worldly possessions.

Sometimes people may be tempted to think of Christianity as a helpful way of obtaining something they want. However, fake faith breaks down easily. Once those people have received what they want, they show no further interest in God. True faith must be focused on God alone.

BIBLE READING

The book of Acts tells the story of a man named Simon who was very much like Crafty, Moneylove, Save-All, and Earthy. He began to follow the apostles because he saw the great miracles they performed. Simon knew that he could make a lot of money if he could do those miracles. Let's read the story:

Now for some time a man named Simon had practiced sorcery in the city and amazed all the people of Samaria. He boasted that he was someone great, and all the people, both high and low, gave him their attention and exclaimed, "This man is rightly called the Great Power of God." They followed him because he had amazed them for a long time with his sorcery.

But when they believed Philip as he proclaimed the good news of the kingdom of God and the name of Jesus Christ, they were baptized, both men and women. Simon himself believed and was baptized. And he followed Philip everywhere, astonished by the great signs and miracles he saw.

When the apostles in Jerusalem heard that Samaria had accepted the word of God, they sent Peter and John to Samaria. When they arrived, they prayed for the new believers there that they might receive the Holy Spirit, because the Holy Spirit had not yet come on any of them; they had simply been baptized in the name of the Lord Jesus. Then Peter and John placed their hands on them, and they received the Holy Spirit.

When Simon saw that the Spirit was given at the laying on of the apostles' hands, he offered them money and said, "Give me also this ability so that everyone on whom I lay my hands may receive the Holy Spirit."

Peter answered: "May your money perish with you, because you thought you could buy the gift of God with money! You have no part or share in this ministry, because your heart is not right before God. Repent of this wickedness and pray to the Lord in the hope that he may forgive you for having such a thought in your heart. For I see that you are full of bitterness and captive to sin."

Then Simon answered, "Pray to the Lord for me so that nothing you have said may happen to me." (Acts 8:9-24)

Simon the Sorcerer was baptized as a Christian, but he seemed most interested in gaining more power for miracles. Simon was accustomed to making money by amazing people with his sorcery, and he thought he had found a new source of power. When he offered to pay Peter to receive the power, however, Peter declared that Simon's heart was not right before God. Peter sternly warned Simon to repent of his wickedness.

Sadly, it appears that Simon the Sorcerer did not learn his lesson. Instead of repenting, he asked Peter to pray that bad things would not happen to him.

CONCLUSION

Can you think of another Bible story in which someone tried to use God to gain money or power? (If you cannot remember one, read pages 106-107 of *Pilgrim's Progress in Today's English*.) Write your example below.

_____

_____

_____

 REMEMBER! Our faith must focus on God alone. We should not view Christianity as a tool to gain money, power, or other worldly things.

PART 2: DEMAS
READ PAGES 107–110.

DO YOU REMEMBER?

Christian met a man named _____ who became his friend

on the journey. They met some hypocrites named _____,

_____, _____, and _____,

who were only interested in _____.

PLACES

What does the name of this hill mean?

Lucre _____

Answer the questions below:

1. What was located inside the hill called Lucre?

_____

2. What happened to people who approached the hill?

_____

3. Who was Demas?

_____

4. What happened to Crafty and his friends?

_____

5. What was written on the Pillar of Salt?

_____

 SYMBOLISM

John Bunyan concludes his discussion on greed with a warning. He shows how people can be drawn away from their faith and destroyed by covetousness. Even Hopeful is nearly persuaded by Demas to wander away from the path looking for riches, and when Crafty and his companions are called aside, they disappear into the pit.

The Pillar of Salt is the final declaration of the dangers of loving riches and other worldly things too much. Genesis 19 tells us that God destroyed the city of Sodom. A man named Lot and his family had been spared by God, but Lot's wife ignored the warning to run without looking back. She looked back at Sodom and became a pillar of salt.

Jesus later used that story as an illustration to warn his followers not to focus on saving their possessions when judgment came upon the land (Luke 17).

BIBLE READING

In the New Testament, Demas was a man who initially followed God and even ministered with the apostles. In the end, however, he deserted the work of God because he loved the world (II Timothy 4:10). The apostle John wrote about the dangers of loving the world in one of his letters:

Do not love the world or anything in the world. If anyone loves the world, love for the Father is not in them. For everything in the world—the lust of the flesh, the lust of the eyes, and the pride of life—comes not from the Father but from the world. The world and its desires pass away, but whoever does the will of God lives forever. (I John 2:15-17)

CONCLUSION

According the passage in I John, what happens to the world and its desires?

_____

What happens to those who do the will of God?

_____

REMEMBER! Greed is dangerous.   Ultimately, it will destroy someone who does not guard against it. We are called to seek first the kingdom of God.

PART 3: GIANT DESPAIR
READ PAGES 110–118.

DO YOU REMEMBER?

Christian and Hopeful approached a hill called _____. A man

named _____ called to them to leave the path and go to the

silver mine. _____ was tempted, but Christian warned him not

listen. Later, _____ , Moneylove, _____, and Earthy

disappeared in the _____ mine. Christian and Hopeful saw a

warning on the Pillar of _____ that said, "Remember Lot's wife."

CHARACTERS

What do these characters' names mean?

Self-Confidence _____

Despair _____

Gloom _____

Answer the questions below:

1. Why did Christian and Hopeful leave the path?

    _____

2. What did Giant Despair do with Christian and Hopeful?

    _____

3. How did Christian and Hopeful escape?

    _____

 SYMBOLISM

Christian and Hopeful became prisoners of Despair when they took the wrong path. They thought it would be an easier way and would not matter much, but soon, they realized they had gone very far astray. Instead of obeying God, they had followed their self-confidence to do things their own way. By the time they realized their error, they were far from the right path.

Despair comes upon us when we realize we have committed some dreadful mistake. Instead of simply repenting and moving on, we can become obsessed with our sin and our trouble. We may feel like we are trapped and cannot escape from the terrible sense of gloom and discouragement.

Christian was kept strong by his friend Hopeful, who reminded him to hope in the Lord. Ultimately, both of them were able to escape by remembering the promises of God.

When we focus on ourselves and our disappointment and mistakes, we will soon begin to feel that we cannot go on. God gives us promises in the Bible so that we may always remember His love for us. Strengthened by the promises, we are able to go on and live as we should.

BIBLE READING

Let's read one of God's promises:

> Love the LORD, all his faithful people! The LORD preserves those who are true to him, but the proud he pays back in full. Be strong and take heart, all you who hope in the LORD. (Psalm 31:23-24)

God promises to sustain those who are true to him and to judge the proud. When we remember this promise, we can be strong and brave. We put our hope in God.

CONCLUSION

Can you think of another promise of God? Find it in your Bible and write it
below:

_____

_____

_____

_____

 REMEMBER!   When we put our hope in God, we will never be
prisoners of despair.

CHAPTER 8: AT THE DELECTABLE MOUNTAINS

> ## THE WARNING OF THE SHEPHERDS
> ### READ PAGES 119–122.

DO YOU REMEMBER?

Christian and Hopeful took the wrong path and followed after a man

named _____ . When they realized they were far away

from the true path, they turned back but were captured by _____.

Imprisoned in the castle, Christian nearly despaired, but _____

encouraged him. Finally, Christian remembered a key called _____,

and they were able to _____.

CHARACTERS

What do these characters' names mean?

Knowledge _____

Experience _____

Watchful _____

Sincerity _____

Answer the questions below:

1. What did Christian and Hopeful see at the bottom of Error Hill?

   _____

2. What did Christian and Hopeful see from Caution Peak?

   _____

3. Who had traveled the byway to Hell?

   _____

4. How did Christian and Hopeful see the Celestial City?

   _____

   _____

5.   As Christian and Faithful were leaving, what final two warnings were they given?

_____

_____

 SYMBOLISM

As we continue our Christian walk every day, we begin to gain experience and understanding. We learn to watch out for certain errors and to persevere in trials. We gain a larger perspective of life which permits us to see dangers more easily.

John Bunyan pictures these aspects of Christian life as shepherds who caution us about pitfalls on the road ahead. It is wise to remember the lessons we have learned, as Christian and Hopeful recalled their experience as prisoners of Giant Despair.

We should also listen to the knowledge and experience of others, as Christian and Hopeful avoided falling from the cliff at Error Hill. They looked at the destruction of people who had gone that way, and so they realized they should never venture down that path.

BIBLE READING

The Bible tells us to be quick to learn, especially from those who have more knowledge and experience:

> The fear of the LORD is the beginning of knowledge, but fools despise wisdom and instruction. Listen, my son, to your father's instruction and do not forsake your mother's teaching. (Proverbs 1:7-8)

Wisdom begins with fearing God and honoring His commands. The writer of Proverbs declares that anyone who hates to be taught is a fool. If we are too proud to learn, then we are doomed to make serious mistakes which could have been easily avoided if we had only listened to knowledge and experience.

CONCLUSION

The passage in Proverbs especially advises us to listen to our parents. Why do you think that is so important?

_____

_____

Good fathers and mothers set rules for their children. These rules are based on the parents' knowledge and experience. Just as the shepherds warned Christian and Hopeful of dangers they would encounter on the way to the Celestial City, parents warn children of dangers in the world. Fathers and mothers want their children to grow up safe and healthy—both physically and spiritually.

Give three examples of rules your parents have set to keep you safe.

1. _____

2. _____

3. _____

 REMEMBER!   Only a fool refuses to learn.

CHAPTER 9: IN THE LOW COUNTRY OF CONCEIT

PART 1: IGNORANCE AND LITTLE-FAITH
READ PAGES 123-126.

DO YOU REMEMBER?

Christian and Hopeful arrived at the _____ Mountains.

They met some _____ who gave them warnings about the

journey ahead. They also caught a glimpse of the _____ City

through a glass called Eye-of- _____ .

CHARACTERS

What do these characters' names mean?

Ignorance _____

Turnaway _____

Little-Faith _____

PLACES

What do these names mean?

Conceit _____

Apostasy _____

Answer the questions below:

1. Why was Ignorance sure he would be accepted at the gate of the Celestial City?

   _____

2. Whom did Christian and Hopeful see led away by demons?

   _____

3. What were the names of the enemies who had overcome Little-Faith?

   _____

4. Why did Christian say that pilgrims must not brag about their courage?

   _____

SYMBOLISM

In this chapter, John Bunyan illustrates the difficulties encountered by Christians who become conceited. When life is easy, people may grow proud. They may feel as though they do not need God anymore.

The first example appears in the character of Ignorance. God's Word declares that salvation is found in Christ alone. Ignorance does not think he needs Christ. He believes he is good enough to be accepted in heaven without repenting of his sins or putting his faith in Jesus. Ignorance does some good works which he believes God will accept as payment for his sins.

The second example is found in the story of Turnaway, who has been captured by demons. Tangled up in terrible sins, Turnaway wanders into darkness. Christian recognizes that Turnaway is from a town called Apostasy. Turnaway is an **apostate**—a person who rejects the true teaching of Scripture. In his pride, he has cast off the Bible as the Word of God. Consequently, he has been ensnared by sin.

Finally, we are told about a man named Little-Faith—a man still on the right path but having lost all his joy in the journey. He is sad, because he does not trust God as he should. Little-Faith put his trust in himself instead of God. When he made some mistakes, he lost all his confidence.

BIBLE READING

We become conceited whenever we trust ourselves for salvation and strength. The Bible tells us to put our hope in God. He is our Savior:

Why, my soul, are you downcast? Why so disturbed within me? Put your hope in God, for I will yet praise him, my Savior and my God. (Psalm 43:5)

If we trust in God, we will not be downcast or disturbed. We know that God is sovereign over everything, and He provides for us.

CONCLUSION

Suppose someone tells you, "I believe that I am good enough to go to heaven because I am usually nice to other people."

How would John Bunyan describe this person? (Think of the name he gave to the character who spoke that way.)

_____

Suppose someone tells you, "I have made so many mistakes. God could never possibly accept me!"

How would John Bunyan describe this person? (Think of the name he gave to the character who grieved over all his mistakes.)

_____

 REMEMBER! Put your trust in God. Only God can save us from our sins, and only God can give us the strength and perseverance we need in life.

PART 2: THE DECEIVER AND THE ATHEIST
READ PAGES 126–129.

DO YOU REMEMBER?

Christian and Hopeful entered the low country of _____. They

met a man named _____ who told them that he was certain to be

accepted to the Celestial City because he was _____ . They also saw

a man named Turnaway, who had been captured by _____, and a

man named _____ who constantly grieved over his loss.

CHARACTERS

What do these characters' names mean?

Deceiver _____

Atheist _____

Answer the questions below:

1. What color were the clothes of the Deceiver? _____

2. What happened to Christian and Hopeful when they followed the Deceiver?

   _____

3. What did the Shining One carry in his hand?

   _____

4. Why were Christian and Hopeful so ashamed of themselves?

   _____

   _____

5. Why did Mr. Atheist laugh at Christian and Hopeful?

   _____

 SYMBOLISM

Christian and Hopeful grow lazy when the road becomes easy. Even though the shepherds have provided them with instructions, they do not properly heed the warning. Because they fail to attend to the words of Knowledge, Experience, and the others, they fall into the net of the Deceiver.

The Bible warns us about deceivers who attempt to lead God's people astray. They are false teachers and false prophets. If Christians are not careful, they can be trapped.

The Shining One who frees Christian and Hopeful chides them for their carelessness. He raises his whip as if to strike them in punishment. This symbolizes God's correction when we fail to listen to the Bible. God's discipline is not intended to be cruel; it reminds us to stay on the right path and to avoid entangling ourselves in sin.

Like the atheist in the story, many people today do not believe God exists. In his pride, Atheist refuses to put faith in anything which does not offer him immediate rewards. He assumes that anyone who believes in God is a fool, and he considers himself very wise. However, Christian and Hopeful realize that Atheist is merely another deceiver.

BIBLE READING

In his epistle to the Galatians, Paul warns God's people to watch out for those who seek to deceive them. He reminds us that we should never listen to anyone whose teachings are not grounded thoroughly in Scripture. Paul also warns us that evil may not appear obviously bad. The deceiver might even look like a messenger straight from heaven! But we should never be deceived:

I am astonished that you are so quickly deserting the one who called you to live in the grace of Christ and are turning to a different gospel— which is really no gospel at all. Evidently some people are throwing you into confusion and are trying to pervert the gospel of Christ. But even if we or an angel from heaven should preach a gospel other than the one we preached to you, let them be under God's curse! As we have already said, so now I say again: If anybody is preaching to you a gospel other than what you accepted, let them be under God's curse! (Galatians 1:6-9)

CONCLUSION

There are many people today who follow false teachers. Often those teachers claim to receive their messages directly from God. We must carefully avoid deceivers.

Suppose someone says to you, "I had a vision of heaven, and now I have a new message from God. You do not need to read the Bible anymore. Just listen to me!"

What should you say?

_____

_____

 REMEMBER! God has warned us that deceivers exist in the world. We must be on guard and hold very tightly to the truth of the gospel.

PART 3: HOPEFUL
READ PAGES 129–137.

DO YOU REMEMBER?

In spite of the warning of the _____ , Christian and Hopeful

followed the _____ . They were caught in a _____ until

the _____ One freed them.

Later, they met a man called _____ who laughed at them for

believing in _____ .

Answer the questions below:

1. Why did Christian refuse to let Hopeful lay down to sleep on the Enchanted Ground?

    _____

2. Why sort of man had Hopeful been before he became a pilgrim?

    _____

3. After Hopeful reformed himself and lived a good life, why did he still feel anxious?

_____

_____

4. Who was Hopeful's friend? _____

5. What new understanding made Hopeful's heart overflow with joy?

_____

_____

 ## SYMBOLISM

Hopeful's sleepiness symbolizes the laziness which may come upon us when Christian life becomes routine. Christian refuses to let Hopeful sleep and recalls his mind to all the reasons he should be thankful to God. Hopeful is able to stay alert and make progress on the path because he recollects God's grace to him.

When Hopeful tells his story, he reveals that he was once very much like Ignorance. He thought he could save himself by simply leaving his sin behind and living a good life. Once Hopeful realized he could not pay for his own sins, he became much like Little-Faith—doubting that God would ever save a sinner who had done such terrible things.

Faithful (before he died) had been a good friend to Hopeful. Faithful told Hopeful about **grace**. He helped Hopeful understand that salvation is a gift from God, not something we can earn by doing good works.

Hopeful's heart filled with joy when he realized that God saves everyone who believes in Christ for salvation. God declares in Scripture that we are saved if we repent and believe, so we should trust that we are indeed saved. God never lies. He is always faithful.

.

BIBLE READING

The Bible tells us that we were all dead in our sins before Christ saved us. None of us could ever earn our salvation through good works:

As for you, you were dead in your transgressions and sins, in which you used to live when you followed the ways of this world and of the ruler of the kingdom of the air, the spirit who is now at work in those who are disobedient. All of us also lived among them at one time, gratifying the cravings of our flesh and following its desires and thoughts. Like the rest, we were by nature deserving of wrath. But because of his great love for us, God, who is rich in mercy, made us alive with Christ even when we were dead in transgressions—it is by grace you have been saved. And God raised us up with Christ and seated us with him in the heavenly realms in Christ Jesus, in order that in the coming ages he might show the incomparable riches of his grace, expressed in his kindness to us in Christ Jesus. For it is by grace you have been saved, through faith—and this is not from yourselves, it is the gift of God— not by works, so that no one can boast. (Ephesians 2:1-9)

Salvation is a gift of God's grace. Christ atoned for our sin—not because we are good, but because God loves us. He saved us while we were still in our sins.

CONCLUSION

The apostle Paul wrote to his friend Timothy about his amazement at God's grace to him. Like Hopeful, Paul had once been a terrible sinner. He rejoiced that God forgave his sins and raised him up to a new life in Christ.

Read Paul's declaration to Timothy in I Timothy 1:15-16. Copy it here:

_____

_____

_____

_____

_____

 REMEMBER! We are saved by grace through faith in Christ.

CHAPTER 10: THE TALK WITH IGNORANCE

> ## PART 1: FALSE FAITH AND TRUE FAITH
> ### READ PAGES 138–142.

DO YOU REMEMBER?

Hopeful almost fell asleep on the _____ ground. Christian

kept Hopeful awake by having him talk about his _____.

Hopeful said he had once been a terrible _____ , but then he

tried to mend his ways. But only when he understood God's _____

was he able to live a _____ Christian life.

Answer the questions below:

1. Why was Ignorance sure that God would accept him?

    _____

    _____

2. Did Ignorance believe that his heart could be deceived?

_____

3. How did Christian respond to Ignorance?

_____

_____

4. Was Ignorance persuaded by Christian?

_____

 ## SYMBOLISM

Many people believe that God will accept them because they are good. They do not understand their own wickedness. They do not like to think about all the bad things they have done. They make excuses for themselves in their hearts, and then they trust their own hearts rather than the Word of God.

Even though Ignorance claims to believe God, he refuses to accept God's Word about himself and his sinful condition. He will not listen to anything that judges him.

Like Christian, we should remember that God's Word is the ultimate standard. We should not listen to our own thoughts and ideas about what is acceptable. Our hearts can deceive us. We must read the Bible and believe that God's Word is true.

BIBLE READING

The book of Proverbs often speaks of mockers—those who refuse to obey God's Word or listen to the warnings of others:

Do not rebuke mockers or they will hate you; rebuke the wise and they will love you. Instruct the wise and they will be wiser still; teach the righteous and they will add to their learning. The fear of the LORD is the beginning of wisdom, and knowledge of the Holy One is understanding. (Proverbs 9:8-10)

In *Pilgrim's Progress*, Ignorance represents a mocker. Unmoved by the instruction of Scripture and the warnings of his Christian friends, he persists in following his own way. He is ignorant because he chooses to be ignorant; he refuses to learn. When Christian and Hopeful attempt to instruct him, he merely becomes annoyed and will not walk with them anymore. Although Ignorance believes himself to be very wise, he acts foolishly.

CONCLUSION

According to Proverbs 9:10, what is the beginning of wisdom?

_____

_____

Ignorance thought he was very wise. Where was he finding his ideas about salvation?

_____

Suppose a man discovers that he is wrong about his ideas and behavior.

If he does not change his ways, is he a wise man? _____

If he changes and begins to do the right thing, is he a wise man? _____

Ignorance refused to walk with anyone who did not think exactly as he did. How does this make him a mocker?

_____

_____

 REMEMBER! God is the source of all true wisdom.

PART 2: BACKSLIDING
READ PAGES 143–147.

DO YOU REMEMBER?

Christian and Hopeful met _____ again, and they tried

to talk with him. Ignorance trusted _____ instead of believing

God's _____ . When he realized Christian and Hopeful did

did not agree with him, Ignorance refused to _____ with them.

CHARACTERS

What do these characters' names mean?

Mr. Temporary _____

Self-Save _____

Answer the questions below:

1. Hopeful tells a story about a man named Temporary. What is the story?

   _____

   _____

   _____

2. Christian speculates that people like Temporary are initially repentant because they fear hell. He says they are like thieves and murderers who weep in front of a judge. They appear repentant, but if the judge releases them so that they are not afraid anymore, what happens?

   _____

 SYMBOLISM

In Christian life, we will occasionally encounter backsliders—people who appear to make a sincere profession of faith in Christ, but then turn away. In the end, they are often more hardened against the teaching of Scripture than those who have never attended church at all.

Christian explains to Hopeful that backsliding is rooted in the motivation for following Christ in the first place. If people are only afraid of going to hell but have no sincere love for God, then their faith will be temporary—here one minute, gone the next. If they can convince themselves that hell is not immediately threatening, they go back to their sins.

People who are honest in their repentance will persevere in faith. Their hearts are changed by the Holy Spirit so that they love God and want to obey the Bible.

BIBLE READING

The apostle Peter warned against backsliding in his letter to believers:

Therefore, dear friends, since you have been forewarned, be on your guard so that you may not be carried away by the error of the lawless and fall from your secure position. But grow in the grace and knowledge of our Lord and Savior Jesus Christ. To him be glory both now and forever! Amen (II Peter 3:17-18)

Peter encourages his fellow Christians to continue to grow in faith so that they will not fall away.

CONCLUSION

Suppose someone says to you, "I never go to church or read my Bible anymore. I used to do all that stuff, but now I just try to be a good person."

How would you respond?

_____

_____

The apostle Peter tells us to continue growing in grace and knowledge of Christ. What are some things you do to grow in your faith?

_____

_____

 REMEMBER! Guard against backsliding, and continue growing in the grace and knowledge of Christ Jesus.

CHAPTER 11: NEAR TO THE CITY OF GOD

CROSSING THE RIVER
READ PAGES 149–156.

DO YOU REMEMBER?

After the talk with Ignorance, _____ and Hopeful

discussed the problem of _____ . They remembered a man

named _____ who had once shown great interest in faith,

but had turned back after meeting _____ .

Answer the questions below:

1. What was the last great obstacle that Christian and Hopeful had to cross in order to reach the Celestial City?

   _____

2. Which of the pilgrims was most frightened by the river?

   _____

3. How did Hopeful encourage Christian?

_____

_____

4. What happened to Hopeful and Christian after they crossed the river?

_____

_____

5. What happened to Ignorance when he reached the gate of the Celestial City?

_____

_____

 ## SYMBOLISM

Many people—even Christians—fear death. They may be afraid that death will sweep them away and destroy them forever. They may wonder whether God will receive them.

Hopeful encourages Christian by reminding him of the promises of God. We do not have to be frightened by death if we put our trust in God. His Word is true and faithful. He forgives our sins and receives us into our eternal home.

Ignorance trusts in himself so much that death does not even trouble him. He is not as frightened as Christian, but in the end, his hope is in vain.

John Bunyan concludes the tale of Christian's journey by reminding us to put our faith in God, not in ourselves. God's promises are always true. He will never forsake us.

BIBLE READING

The writing in letters of gold on the Celestial City is a reference to one of the promises found in the book of Revelation:

Blessed are those who wash their robes, that they may have the right to the tree of life and may go through the gates into the city. (Revelation 22:14)

The phrase **wash their robes** refers to repentance of sin. People who repent and believe in Christ are given the right to the blessings of heaven. God has promised this to us, and we may trust that God's Word is true.

CONCLUSION

There are many Bible verses which promise us eternal life. Can you remember another one? Write it below:

REMEMBER! You do not need to be afraid of death when you put your faith in God.

Made in the USA
Monee, IL
01 October 2022

15019909R00083